IMAGES of WEST BANK

Fiona Jenkins

Festival of Britain Queen Lily Tiernan and attendants, Parsonage Road, 1951

Boys outside The Parochial Hall, Davies Street, 1930's

Morris dancers for St. Mary's Church Rose Queen celebrations, Viaduct Street, 1930s.

IMAGES of WEST BANK

Fiona Jenkins

Published by:
West Bank Heritage Project,
c/o 188 Ditchfield Road,
Widnes.
WA8 8JY

First Published 2005

© Copyright West Bank Heritage
  Project, 2005

Front Cover Image:
Betty Knight, Jean Percival and Joan
Percival walking along Oakland Street,
c1954

Back Cover Images:
The Band Stand, Victoria Gardens, c1900
Morris Dancers, Viaduct Street, c1930s
Ladies and girl sat on The Promenade
wall, c1934

End pages reproduced from a 1938
Ordinance Survey map.

Typesetting and origination by:
West Bank Heritage Project

Printed by:
Biddles Ltd,
24 Rollesby Road,
Hardwick Industrial Estate,
Kings Lynn,
Norfolk.
PE30 4LS
UK

ISBN 0-9550509-0-1

Members of St. Mary's Church Youth Group, The Parochial Hall, Davies Street, c1950

Contents

Acknowledgements

We are grateful for the support and contribution of those who loaned photographs and memorabilia and/or shared their memories and knowledge with the West Bank Heritage Project:

Maureen Taylor, Helen Symthe, Megan Jones, Cath and Leo Nolan, Josie Carney, Jean Mottram, Bill Foster, Wallace and Muriel Woods, Rita and John Moss, Ron Dennett, Dot Millar, Joyce Cowley, Tommy Wilkinson, Wendy and Dennis Malone, Chris Adams Keith Andrews, Arnold Walker, Terry Bums, Ron Girvin, John Harper, Roy Hayes, John and Cecilia McMullen, John Yates, Margery Lewis, Dorothy and Alan Mercer, Alf Burgess, Marjorie Fallen, Judith Gelling, John Tully, Ray Fenney, Peter Cox, Pauline Ruth, Eric Smith, Doreen Angus, Eunice Stobbie, Ron Cank, Cath Condron, Kathleen Kelleher, Edna Millington, Richard Myler, Graham Ewell, Val Angus, Lillian Woodstock, Megan Weir, Linda Blease, Bob Martindale, Philip Johnson, James Glynn, Ernie Roscoe, William Johnson, John and Ruth Garaghty, Ann Wall, George Wareing, Francis Ireland, Vivian Batty, Cathie Miller, Annette Quirk, Rene Jones, Gwen Nuttie, Violet Nuttie, Harold Wadsworth, Mary Halliburton, Jean Murray, Eunice Robertson, Tom Cobley, Diana Potter, Gordon Gilray, Graham Earl, Mamie Gilhooley, Mike Flynn, May Thomas, Mr David Follows, Edith Heesom, Stanley Ellison, Laura Burton, Mary Halliburton, Alma Lowe, Kath Stevens, Nita Greenleaves, Liz and Bill Johnson, Mrs Naylor, and other private contributors some whom wished to remain anonymous in this publication.

We would also wish to thank Halton Borough Transport, ICI, Widnes Weekly News and the Industrial Railway Society for their permission to reproduce images which have been loaned by the above persons.

The West Bank Heritage Project and this book would not have occurred without the inspiration and dedication of Project Co-ordinator John Yates and the commitment and enthusiasm of the members of the Project Steering Group: Rev. Ray Jones (Chair), Alison Gleave (Development Officer, Halton Voluntary Action), Adele Clarke (Development Officer, Halton Borough Council) and David Angus (Churchwarden).

Further thanks goes to the following for their support and encouragement: Widnes World, the staff and children of West Bank School, the staff at Catalyst Science Discovery Centre, Elsie and Ted Gleave

We would also like to thank everyone who volunteered to help at the exhibition at St. Mary's Church, West Bank in September 2004 as well as those who assisted in its preparation. Particular thanks go to Maire Knight, Louise Mitchell, Lewis Redhead, Bronwyn Davies, Graham Earl, Maureen Fahey and Christine Allison. This exhibition would not have been possible without the support of a grant from the Heritage Lottery Fund.

This publication would not have been possible without the funding from the Community Foundation for Merseyside and the Community Chest grant scheme which they operate. They therefore receive our grateful thanks.

Foreword by Rt. Hon Lord Ashley of Stoke, C.H.

All too often the rich and fascinating lives of local communities are allowed to pass unrecognised and unrecorded, to our great detriment. The West Bank community was as interesting, indeed fascinating, as any and undoubtedly deserves this book.

Its main lifeblood was derived from local people and successive generations had lived there for many years. To these vigorous and industrious people was added the influx of lively and eager families from places like Ireland, Poland and Lithuania. The problems of assimilation are never easy, especially if religious differences arise, yet they mixed agreeably with the locals and soon became part of the fabric of West Bank. The remarkable energy and skill of these people is perhaps best symbolised by renowned rugby footballers like Vince Karaulius, an outstanding international player who, on overseas tour in South America, was called the "Wild Bull of the Pampas."

Such driving energy was needed by anyone settling in West Bank because work in the factories was hard. Timber, copper, soap and chemicals were the main industries of Widnes, supported by a wide range of other factories. The smells of the many ICI chemical factories were part of daily life, though in West Bank, these were softened by the smells of Gossages soap factory.

A common sight in West Bank was to see women scrubbing the front door step and even washing down the pavement outside their homes. These house-proud people washed their clothes by hand - they had no washing machines in the early days - and used a "dolly tub", a glorified stool with a long handle in the centre and a cross bar at the top to turn the clothes. Then they would go to their various churches and worship.

To capture the lives and the environment of these people is no mean achievement. This book will be read with avid interest by all who have experienced the proud values of West Bank.

Jack Ashley

16th November 2004

Morris dancers Mabel Gelling and Doreen Hall, 75 Chomondeley Street, 1930's

Introduction

West Bank: *"A Poor and Honest but Loving Community"*

Marjorie Fallon, West Banker, 2004

This book seeks to provide 'snap shots' of West Bank people and places revealing, over the decades, the unique, rich and diverse heritage of this Widnes community. It is the result of a successful Heritage Lottery Funded project to celebrate the past of the people who lived in this close knit community and worked in the midst of the chemical industry on the banks of the River Mersey.

The aim of the project was to gather together images, memorabilia and memories associated with West Bank by appealing to the public to delve into their attics, drawers and cupboards and loan us their private collections so that a picture of the changing life of the community could be the life seen though the eyes of it's inhabitants. In this working class area with little disposable income for luxuries like cameras until well into the late 20th Century, and comparatively few photographs exist when compared to more prosperous areas. West Bankers would have visited photographers studios like Lautenburgs, in Waterloo Road or paid one of the travelling photographers who went around knocking on West Bank doors, in order to obtain a portrait of a family member. Photographs of everyday life and how local and national events affected West Bankers were therefore rare in their day and today, where they exist, remain scattered in private family albums.

A 'lost' history of West Bank has, therefore, lain unseen except by a lucky few. As told through photographs, this history largely appears one of happy times because, after all, it is human nature to want to record these occasions rather than sadder times. Nevertheless, if the reader is to look closely, there are some which do give a glimpse of the hard times, which the West Bank community has lived through over the last 100 years or so. Indeed the memories attached to the photographs often came with stories of happy times amongst the social and economic hardships faced by West Bankers. This story, as told by pictures and memories, of the community was at risk of becoming lost. It needed to be captured, safeguarded for the future and shared.

A digital archive of images has therefore been created to permanently preserve West Bank history. Many former and current West Bankers and those with West Bank associations contacted us and an overwhelming 900 images were collected in total. Many of these images were displayed in the Heritage Festival Exhibition held in September 2004 at St. Mary's Church. Some of these were collected too late to use in the exhibition itself and were brought in as people became inspired by the display in the days, weeks and months which have followed. This publication has therefore not only allowed us to include those used in the exhibition but also a great many more previously unseen. These include photographs in streets which were previously unrepresented as well as other activities and events taking place on West Bank. It is due to the generosity, time and effort of people who loaned us their photographs, memorabilia and spoke of their recollections, that the following pages are filled with such interesting and important records of West Bank life. By the photographs, objects and stories which you, the public, have provided you have presented and preserved the history of life on West Bank for future generations.

Fiona Jenkins,
Project Development Officer,
The West Bank Heritage Project.
May 2005

"The way of life has gradually changed over the years and now West Bank is a small village to what it used to be. [It's] still a village with its own special character, and not a bad place to live in, and thank God gone are the obnoxious smells and the terrible poverty."
Marjorie Fallon, West Banker, 2004

**A steam engine belonging to R. Rathbone and Sons,
contractors of Atherton near Mancheter, St. Mary's Road, c1900**
On close inspection of this photograph the railway bridge can be seen in the background but the Transportor Bridge has yet to be built.

Chapter One

Home Life

**Nancy, Norman and Jane Hanson and Elizabeth Thompson.
74 St. Mary's Villa's Beamont Street, 1964**

"The houses on West Bank had what we called a 'back kitchen' where we cooked and there was a pantry. Our kitchen, which was really our living room I suppose, had a pulley on the ceiling for washing, a sideboard, a high mantelpiece and chairs. We also had a parlour which was smaller and was reserved for best. Upstairs there were two bedrooms. In the backyard there was a boiler, coal house and outside toilet."
Wallace Woods, 19 West Street, 1930s.

"The square patch of pavement in front of the door was washed and then whitened with donkey stone every day."
Elsie Gleave, West Banker, 1930s

Left: **Margaret Wilkinson, corner of Irwell and Viaduct Street, 1948/9**

"Our washing had to be dried inside and the kitchen and the back kitchen would be steaming with the clothes, hanging from the pulleys in the ceiling, which were dripping wet."
Elsie Gleave, West Banker, 1930s

Right: **Laura and David Mercer, backyard 17 James Street, 1930s**

Dennis Malone, 44 Church Street, 1945

Built in the late 19th Century West Bank houses did not have a bathroom, only an outside toilet. Tin baths were filled with a jug or bucket using water from the boiler in the backyard.

It was not unusual for many families to take in lodgers to help make ends meet. When this photograph was taken there were 12 people spanning three generations living at this house. Living with, or very close to, immediate and/or an extended family was not uncommon.

Left: **Mrs Sophia Turton with one of her lodgers, Noreen Clancey from Ireland, 44 Church Street, 1947**

**Mrs Cank, holding Beryl,
with Thomas and Ron
40 Beamont Street, 1929**

*"We had no electric lighting until the mid
1930's, before that we just had gas lighting.
Downstairs we had mantles but upstairs we
just had the bar jet,"*
Ron Cank, West Banker, 1930s

**John Wilkinson with Ivy Tomlinson,
Viaduct Street, 1948/49**

Left: **Ada Nash and baby,
23 St. Mary's Road, c1913**

"From the back door into the yard, the wash house and the coal shed doors appeared on the left and at the bottom of the yard was the toilet; a fearful place which was very cold in winter." Ruth Halle, describing a house in Mersey Road, 1950s

Left: **Sam Moss and Daughter-in-law Doris Moss, backyard 12 James Street or 45 Irwell Street, 1937**

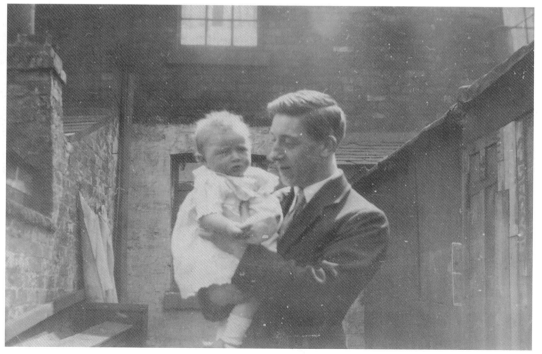

Man and child in a backyard, Wright Street, 1929

**Backyard of a house in Nelson Street
c1900s**

**Walter Motteram and Rinty,
backyard 3 James Street, 1950s**

**Matilda and Tommy Ellis,
backyard 12 Irwell Street, c1910**

**Mrs McCaffery, Joe, Nancy and Michael Miller,
entry way 74 Beamont Street, 1958**

**Dennis Malone and Biddy Holihan
entry way, West Bank c1950**

**Maud Turton, waving, with Mrs
Lawley behind her, entry way behind
her shop, 44 Church Street 1950s**

Mr Tom Ellis, 12 Irwell Street, 1930s
West Bank front doors were solid, decorated by panelling and had huge door knobs in the centre.
"Most people had a piece or lump of glass as a stopper for the door."
Leo Nolan, West Banker, 1940s

Vivien Canning, 7 Beech Terrace, c1950

**Mary and Ken McDermot and baby,
87 Pear Street c1947/8**
Many doors had decorative letter boxes
such as this one.

**Jesse Woodstock,
5 White Street, c1920s**

**Bill and Maud Foster,
38 James Street, c1934**

**From left to right: Charlie, Lucy, Tom
and Mary McGloin, 33 Pitt Street,
c1914**

Such decorative net curtains could be seen in every home on West Bank and were typically found in working class homes. They were less expensive than full length ones and let more light into the rooms of a terrace house whilst still providing privacy.

**From left to right Katy,
Maggie and Jenny Snelson,
West Bank, c1900**

Interior of 22 Davies Street, c1929

Children gathered together for a birthday party. This photograph in the collection is special since it reveals much about the decoration inside a typical West Bank home of the late 1920's. Many more photographs taken outside exist, possibly because taking them outside in natural light was preferable given the limited technology of cameras.

"From the front door, to the right, was a door leading to the parlour although we were not allowed to go into this plushly decorated room. The kitchen was whitewashed with nothing but a cooker, white stone belfast sink with drainer and kitchen cabinet."
Ruth Halle, describing
a house in Mersey Road
1950s

**Mrs Jessie McFarland,
34 James Street, c1960s**

This photograph reflects a typical West Bank lounge of the 1960's. Taken on their 25th wedding anniversary this couple are surrounded by the furniture and rugs that they acquired during their married life.

James and Annie Bernie, 46 Church Street, 1964

Mrs Hunt pictured at her last home on West Bank. She was born on West Bank and lived most of her life in the community in various rented houses. Until fairly recently the majority of West Bankers rented accommodation and often moved just a few doors or streets away as their family grew or the owner of the house wanted to sell it.

Right: **Agnes Hunt,**
　　　82 Church Street,
　　　1960s

Chapter Two

Leisure

Friends in Victoria Gardens, c1938
From left to right: Alf Burgess, Harry Sutton, Harry Bibby, Marjorie Young and Elsie Ford

The Beach, The Promenade and Victoria Gardens

Participants of sports day fun, The Bandstand, Victoria Gardens, 1926

"Every August Bank holiday on the beach and sands there was a fete, it was fantastic (weather permitting). There was a sandcastle building competition, a greasy pole with pieces of ham or beef on the top, they had to climb to get it and did they try!
Marjorie Fallon, West Banker, 1920s

"On the Sands first thing in the morning we used to start sandcastle building, then when it got to the afternoon, there was a yacht race"
Lucy Jones, West Banker, 1920s

"You had to watch carefully for the change in the tide. We would see the first wave come up and splash and dance about but when the second wave came up you had to start to move off the sands."
Linda Kilshaw, West Banker, 1920s

Sandcastle building on Widnes Beach, c1910s

People watching an event from The Prom and Widnes Beach, c1900s

View of people enjoying themselves on West Bank Beach, c1930s

"The Prom was a popular area for women to meet and chat whilst watching their children play. Weekends saw mothers carrying chairs down to The Promenade to await the tide to turn and produce wonderful stretches of yellow sand right up to the Manchester Ship Canal. Many's the time we walked across without getting our feet wet."
Bill Foster, West Banker, 1930s

Left: **Women and children and the sands of West Bank, c.1940s**

Children sat on the rocks beneath The Promenade Wall, 1949
From left to right: Jean Beadsmore, Connie Roscoe, Hazel Roscoe, Pam Rhodes and Ernie Roscoe.

Mrs Hilda Edge, Mrs Kirkbride and friends, The Promenade Wall, 1934
"You could sit on the wall and watch Gossages big boats and the small fishing boats come up the river."
Linda Kilshaw, West Banker, 1920s

Harry Davies, Margaret Kilshaw, Martin, Linda and Arthur Blease, Victoria Gardens, 1958

Above: **Cathie Miller, Victoria Gardens, July 1958**

Left: **Emma McMullen, Victoria Gardens, 1936**

Kath Horabin, Victoria Gardens, 1959

The Century Cinema

The Demolition of the Century Cinema, West Street, c1970s

'The Cennie' as it was affectionately known, was built in 1922. It had 486 seats and a 16 foot screen. The first films that it showed were 'In the Trail of Carvan' and 'The Rescuing Angel'. The films were changed on a Monday and Thursday.

"I used to go mainly to the matinees at 'The Cennie' when I was a girl. It was 3d. I used to enjoy just listening to the pianist playing to accompany the film. His name was Ben Owens, I think, I thought he was fantastic. He used to speed up the music and play very fast and then go slower in relation to what was going on in the film."
Marjorie Fallon, West Banker, 1920s

Performances

Zion Sunday School production of Cinderella, 1938

"Mam made the Prince and Dandini's costumes and, I think, there was some consternation when it was realised that we were going to wear typical principal boy costumes with very brief panties and not the knickerbocker types that they were expecting. The panto was a sell out, a huge success and I would like to think it was because of the leg show!"
Linda Kilshaw, Dandini, 1938

Coachmen and 'pumpkin' coach from a production of Cinderella, Zion Methodist Chapel Sunday School, c1945

The cast of Zion Methodist Chapel Sunday School production of Cinderella, Oakland Street, c1945

Widnes Catholic Operatic Society production of the Mikardo, St. Patrick's Church Hall, Dock Street, 1950s

**Young Person's Group, Nativity Play, St. Mary's Parochial Hall,
Davies Street, 1950s**

**Young Person's Group dressed as Romany Gypsies,
St. Mary's Parochial Hall, Davies Street, 1950s**

Dancing

Sequence Dancing, Zion Methodist Chapel, Oakland Street, 1978

Above: **West Banker John Girvin, the drummer for H. Girvin's Celebrity Dance Band, 1920s**

Dances on West Bank were mainly organised by the churches or factories. West Bankers often ventured into Widnes, to places like the Boro' Hall off Victoria Road, or they went across on The Transporter or footbridge to Runcorn for dances.

Left: **A dance programme, St. Patrick's Church Hall, 1946**

Rugby

West Bank Dock Rugby Team, The yard of the White Star Hotel, 1920s

A rugby team assumed to be from William Gossages, Mersey Road c1920

The Wembley Team Coach on the Road Bridge Approach Road, 1964
The crowd cheer as the team return victorious. Amoung the players are West Bankers Wally Hurstfield, from Hutchinson Street and team captain Vincent Karalius.

Gambling on 'The Cut'

'The Cut', 1970s
On 'The Cut', today's Spike Island, men played the illegal gambling game Pitch and Toss.
"There must have been 40 or 50 men down there gambling their wages. They were gathered by the lock keepers house. Like many boys I kept a look out for any coppers by where the path to the Catalyst Science Discovery Centre is now."
John Yates, West Banker, 1940s

Public Houses

View of the Bridge Hotel, 'The Round House', Church Street. 1955
There were another eight pubs on West Bank besides this one, when this photograph was taken. These were The Arch Hotel (The Slutch'Ole), The Angel, The Main Top, The Vaults, The Mersey Hotel (The Snig), The Swan, The Britannia (The Blood Tub) and The White Star.

A view of the Mersey Hotel, Mersey Road, 1930s
Not only was 'The Snig' a popular drinking venue but it also had a bowling green.

Sailing

A crowd watching a boat on the Mersey from the beach, 1900s

The Mersey was a busy river and watching the hustle and bustle was a popular past time on West Bank. Often there were races on the river and perhaps one of them was going on when this photograph was taken.

Tommy and David Ellis on 'The Excel', the shore of the Mersey, 1920s

These men sailed in any spare time they had. Sometimes they went fishing or shrimping.

'The Sirdar', the River Mersey, 1930s/40s
This pleasure boat was owned and sailed by Mr William Andrews of West Bank.

Above and left :
**The Crew of 'The Marguerite',
The Mersey, c1920s**

T.E Lewis (above marked with a cross) was a West Banker and member of The Mersey Yacht Club who sailed in many competions. He won the club's silver cup five times and as a result it was awarded to him permanently.

A Days Holiday

Victorian ladies on a day trip from West Bank c1880s

On the back row, fourth from the left, is Elizabeth Nestor who was the wife of the first park keeper on West Bank.

"There used to be a day trip organised by the people in Davies Street or James Street every year. It was very popular. I can remember a trip to New Brighton. We caught the bus to Liverpool and went over on the ferry. It was a great treat to do that. When we arrived there was a 'bathing beauty' competition, a fair and a swimming pool on The Prom."
Marjorie Fallon, West Banker, 1920s.

West Bank ladies on a day trip, location Unknown, c1900
First from the left is Catherine Davies and next to her Sarah Jane Malone (nee Davies).

A group of West Bankers in a charabanc, c1920
Few West Bankers could afford to take time off work to have a holiday for a whole week or longer so a day trip in a 'chara' or by train and later by coach was the order of the day. Day trips were often organised by the churches and companies on West Bank or by neighbours from a particular street getting together.

Tom, Matilda and Doris Ellis on a day trip to the Marshes, c1920s
Closer to home West Bank Marshes, Frodsham Hill and Hale Bank were popular destinations.

The Moss family, St. Helens Canal, c1920s

Coach trippers from St. Patrick's Church, Dock Street, c1953

A coach party of West Bankers on a day trip to Southport, c1960s
Southport, Blackpool and New Brighton were popular destinations for day trips as they were not to far away. It is easy to forget that before the arrival of the chemical industry in the mid 19th Century, day trippers from Liverpool travelled to the area of West Bank for their days holiday.

Chapter Three

Worship

**Reverend Geoffery Richens conducts a service from the open air pulpit,
St. Mary's Church grounds, 1960s**

"I used to go to the children's meetings in the mission hall and when we all sat down, Sister Moulton used to say to us "draw Swords" and we all had to hold our bibles in the air." Marjorie Fallon, St Mary's Church, 1920's

"On the very top floor at Hartland there was a full-sized billiard table, which had been used to encourage young men to go there and play, meet and drink tea rather than go to the pub. It was very much a temperance chapel. The room was still fully rigged out with cue rests and scoreboards when I was young." Roy Hayes, Hartland Chapel, 1950s

St. Mary's Church

The old St. Mary's Church, Waterloo Road, c1890s.
The church was built in 1858 and by 1901 the effects of being built on chemical waste were beginning to show as the walls became unstable.

The beginnings of St Mary's Church, c1908
In order to build the church 43 houses had to be knocked down on the new site and over £11, 000 was raised to pay for it.

Leslie Hufton and the foundation stone, St. Mary's Church, 1908
The stone was laid by Mrs F. H. Gossage on 14th May 1908.

The building of the walls, St. Mary's Church, 1908

St. Mary's Church with the tower under construction, c1909

"The noble tower will stand four-square to every wind that blows and will look over to the steeple at Runcorn and not be ashamed."

Bishop of Liverpool, 1908.

The choir outside St. Mary's Church c1910

Bert Bennett, the second choir boy from the left on the second row, sang the first solo when the new church opened.

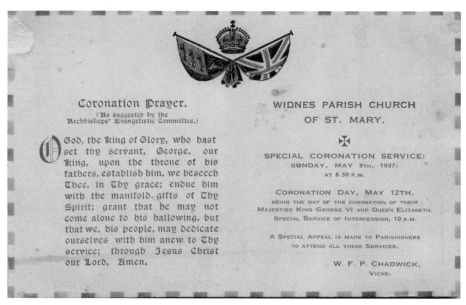

Coronation Prayer.
(As suggested by the
Archbishops' Evangelistic Committee.)

O God, the King of Glory, who hast set thy servant, George, our King, upon the throne of his fathers, establish him, we beseech Thee, in Thy grace; endue him with the manifold gifts of Thy Spirit; grant that he may not come alone to his hallowing, but that we, his people, may dedicate ourselves with him anew to Thy service; through Jesus Christ our Lord, Amen.

WIDNES PARISH CHURCH
OF ST. MARY.

SPECIAL CORONATION SERVICE:
SUNDAY, MAY 9TH, 1937:
AT 6.30 P.M.

CORONATION DAY, MAY 12TH,
BEING THE DAY OF THE CORONATION OF THEIR
MAJESTIES KING GEORGE VI AND QUEEN ELIZABETH.
SPECIAL SERVICE OF INTERCESSION, 10 A.M.

A SPECIAL APPEAL IS MADE TO PARISHIONERS
TO ATTEND ALL THESE SERVICES.

W. F. P. CHADWICK,
VICAR.

**An invitation to attend a special coronation celebration service,
St. Mary's Church, 1937.**

Christmas Card, St. Mary's Church, 1938

St. Marys Church, c1950s

"If you were late going in on a Sunday night when I was in my youth, Mother and I would end up on the back row as all the seats were taken."

Marjorie Fallon, West Banker, 1920s

St. Mary's Rose Queens and Parades

Dorothy Gelling, Rose Queen, 1938
Dorothy was Rose Queen the year that King George VI and Queen Elizabeth visited Widnes.

Lillian Walker, Rose Queen, 1951
Lillian was Rose Queen amid the festivities for The Festival of Britain.

Margaret Mercer, Rose Queen, 1952
Margaret was Rose Queen the year that the old vicarage in Parsonage Road was demolished in preparation for construction of the Runcorn-Widnes Road Bridge.

Wendy Garner, Rose Queen, 1960
Wendy was Rose Queen in the year of St. Mary's Jubilee and a £6,000 Church restoration plan had just been completed.

Margaret Gelling, Rose Queen, 1958
Margaret was Rose Queen in the centenary year of the foundation of the parish of Widnes and the National School.

Diane Tuscott, Mary Queen, 1961

Diane was Rose Queen in the year that the Runcorn-Widnes Road Bridge was opened by
H.R.H Princess Alexandra.

Rose Queen, Colleen Davies, 1964

Colleen was Rose Queen the year that Widnes Rugby League Team beat Hull Kingston
Rovers 13-5 on May 9th at the Challenge Cup Final at Wembley Stadium with Vincent
Karalius, a West Banker, as captain of the team.

Rose Queen Linda Howsley, 1974
Linda was Rose Queen in the year that Zion Methodist Chapel celebrated its centenary.

Rose Queen Michelle Wier, 1980
St. Mary's church celebrated its 70th anniversary in the year that Michelle was Rose Queen.

St. Mary's Sunday School Parade, 1900s

Walking processions were huge events in the life of the church and on these occsaions crowds of West Bankers would line the streets to see the festivities.

Parade of St. Mary's Church congregation, St. Mary's Road, 1950s

St. Mary's Church parade, c1960s

The congregation listen to a sermon given by Reverend Richens, 1960s
Mr Sutton Timmis, a major donor to the new church appeal in 1907, envisaged the building of a unique stone pulpit *"for use on warm evenings and for open air services"*.

St. Patrick's Church

Above Left: **The interior of St.Patrick's Church when a May Queen Service is being held, 1949**

Above Right: **Father McGlade and Altar Boy Billy Unsworth, St. Patrick's Church, c1950s**

Left: **Father McGlade in the Pulpit, St. Patricks Church, c1950s**

Ladies who attended church, St. Patrick's, 1920s
Amongst the ladies are Mary Manning, Kitty Turner, Connie O'Brien and the Eccelson Sisters. There are many Polish parishioners amongst St. Patrick's congregation as well as Lithuanians, Irish immigrants and their descendants.

Girls celebrating their First Holy Communion, c1940s
Fathers Hayes and Strizaker and two missionaries are pictured with the girls.

Boys and girls celebrating their First Holy Communion, St. Patrick's, 1955
The children are pictured with their teachers from St. Patrick's School; Rose May Bill,
Brian Higgins, John McMullen and Frank Moran.

Cecilia and Theresa O'Brien, Irwell Street, 1942

"After the boys and girls had received their first communion in Mass there used to be a celebration... In the staff room, at school, a celebration breakfast was laid on."
Marie Thompson, West Banker, 1940

Helen Myler, 'The Cut', 1941/42

A crowd celebrating the Children's First Holy Communion, West Bank, 1970s

St. Patrick's May Queen's and Processions

Children of Mary procession, St. Patrick's Church, 1956
The Children of Mary was a group for teenage girls who met on Sunday evenings for dicussions with the priest and for social activities.

A May Walk passes St. Patrick's Church, 1930s/40s
These walks amongst West Bank continued well into the 1960's.

A May Walk, West Bank c1930s/1940s

A May Walk behind Dock Street, May 1948

West Bankers watch Therese McCann carrying the banner for the procession as it makes its way around West Bank.

A May Queen and attendants at the altar to Our Lady, St. Patrick's, c1930s

May Queen Theresa Carolan with attendants Irene O'Neil and Theresa McGeiver, St. Patrick's Church, c1946

Cecilia Carolan crowning the statue of The Blessed Virgin Mary, St. Patrick's, Church, 1951

**May Walks decorations on Boltons
Factory gates, Pitt Street, c1950s**

**St. Patrick's May walk,
Milton Street or Pear Street, c1950.**

**Phyllis McCann is the banner bearer for
the May Walk, Wright Street, c1947**

*"It was wonderful as it was the first time
we had a procession since the war. All the
streets were decorated. It was very difficult to get material then. My dress was
made by Calverts, a well known Widnes
shop, and it had swansdown all around
it. They displayed it in the window of the
shop before I wore it."*
Cecilia, McMullen, May Queen, 1951

*"In the month of May we would have 'The
May Walks' where we would process from
the church around West Bank. The May
Queen would lead carrying Our lady
and the children of May and St. Patrick's
School children would follow. The children of Mary would be dressed in blue
and white and the kerbs of the road would
be coloured in blue and white too."*
John Garaghty, St. Patrick's Church
member, 1930s

Hartland Wesleyan Methodist Chapel

The construction of Hartland, Oakland Street, c1872

Other Non-Conformist chapels constructed on West Bank included Trinity Chapel of the Primitive Methodists built in1894 in Waterloo Road and a Welsh Wesleyan Chapel in Cromwell Street.

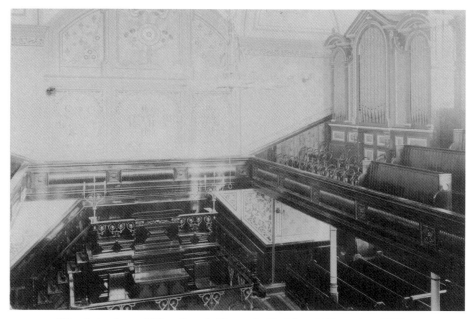

The interior of Hartland Chapel, Oakland Street, c1930s

Above: **The Bright Hour Group, Hartland, 1960s**
Around the table clockwise from front left is Gertrude Highfield, Florence Povey, Jessie McCaffery, Jessie McFarland, Gert Brookfield and Mrs O'Neil.

Left: **A Hartland Chapel Book Mark, 1929**

The Congregation at Hartland, 1973
A special centenary service and a 'Young persons' service of song' marked the occasion.

Zion United Methodist Chapel

A celebration at Zion Chapel, c1900s
The Church opened in 1874. The interior and exterior was much plainer than Hartlands

A wedding breakfast at Zion Chapel, Oakland Street, c1900s

A minister and church wardens from Zion Chapel, c1930s

Interior of Zion Chapel with a sequence dance taking place, 1978
On Thursday evenings many West Bankers would attend the weekly sequence dance.

Interior of Zion Chapel with a badminton match taking place, 1978
Wednesday night was badminton night.

Chapter Four

Celebrations

**Street party celebration for either The Festival of Britain, 1951
or the Coronation of Queen Elizabeth II, Wright Street, 1953**

Royal Occasions

Street decorations for the coronation of Edward VII and Queen Alexandra, Mersey Road, 1903

King George V's trip on the Transporter, 1925

Residents including Mrs Hunt and Edna Hunt, foreground on right hand side, celebrating the Silver Jubilee of George V, James Street, 1935

A street celebration to honour the reigning monarch, James Street, c1936
On close examination the banner in this photograph appears to honour Edward VIII. As he was never crowned King of England then the celebrations can not be for his coronation. Perhaps this photograph was taken amid festivities for his succession.

Street decorations for the coronation of George VI, James Street, 1937

"I woke up one morning and the whole street was decorated, that's how it seemed to me as a child anyway. It was magical. Every house had an arch decorated with red, white and blue and bunting was tied across the street from one bedroom window to another. I can remember standing in the doorway and thinking 'wow!'."

Alan Mercer, West Banker, 1937

A street celebration for the coronation of George VI and Queen Elizabeth, James Street, 12th May 1937

**The street decorated with flags to celebrate the coronation of George VI,
James Street, 1937**

**Laura and David Mercer in their
doorway decorated for the
corononation of Queen Elizabeth II,
James Street, 1953**

**Doorways decorated for the coronation
of Queen Elizabeth II, St. Mary's Villas,
Beamont Street, 1953**

Thelma Wareing, A Coronation Queen, with other children celebrating the coronation of Elizabeth II, 73 Church Street, 1953

Thelma Wareing as a Coronation Queen with attendants, The Bridge Hotel, junction of Viaduct and Church Street, 1953

West Bankers celebrating the coronation of Queen Elizabth II, James Street, 1953
Residents of West Bank decorated barrels with red, white and blue paper and used them
as the support for poles to carry the yards of bunting that festooned the streets.

Neighbours celebrating the coronation of Queen Elizabeth II, 1953
The Queen's coronation was at the dawn of the age of television and any West Bankers
who possessed one were sure to have a full house that day.

Crowds await the arrival of the Queen Mother, outside Parnell's Shop, Mersey Road, 1958

The Queen Mother's visit included a crossing on The Transporter. Her previous visit to Widnes had been with her husband, King George VI in 1938.

A street party for the Silver Jubilee of Queen Elizabeth's coronation, Church Street, 1977

Queen Elizabeth II on West Bank, Spike Island, 1979

"The Y.T.S. (Youth Training Scheme) built a viewing platform for The Queen to stand on with Tablets about the town. People made a tremendous effort to welcome her and made paper flowers and put them in the trees as it was the wrong time of year for flowers. Spike Island had gone from being a busy water highway to becoming disused and derelict but was now a green area the likes of which had never been seen before on West Bank."
Ted Gleave, West Banker and Mayor, 1979

Children from St. Patrick's School having seen the Queen, Spike Island, 1979

The Festival of Britain

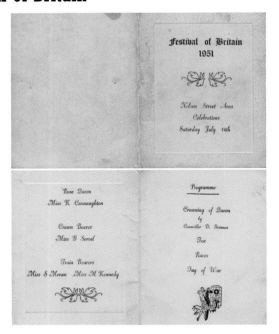

Cecelia Carolan, Eileen and Pat Bernie and a friend, outside 'The Round House' Church Street, 1951

A programme from the Nelson Street area celebrations, 1951

Widnes had a carnival parade almost two miles long

Festival Queen procession, Nelson Street, 1951

Cath Connaughton is pictured here before her crowning ceremony as her crown bearer, Miss Sorvel, leads the party.

Children on the Nelson Street Festival of Britain Float, Nelson Street, 1951
"There was a Welsh girl, a Scottish girl, an English girl, an Irish girl and John Bull on the float I was on. I was the Welsh girl. It was the Mersey Road float which was organised by Povey's shoe shop on Mersey Road. The float was decorated in red, white and blue."
Megan Jones, Mersey Road Float, 1950's

The Nelson Street Festival of Britain Float, Nelson Street, 1951
Mrs Pichilingi watches the festivities whilst resting on her broom. The Bank Street float, 'kaleidoscope', entered into the procession by Mrs Mew won 1st Prize.

Children celebrating the Festival of Britain, Nelson Street, 1951

A street party celebrating the Festival of Britain, 1951
The children of Nelson Street tuck into party food before the races and a tug of
war were held.

**Children in fancy dress,
Viaduct Street, 1951**

**Vivian Canning (left) and a friend
Viaduct Street, 1951**

Children on a Festival of Britain float, Parsonage Road, 1951

Festival of Britain procession passing West Bank School, 'The Birdcage', 1951

Festival of Britain morris dancers near West Bank School, 'The Birdcage', 1951

Events and Festivals

Children Celebrating Empire Day, West Bank School, Oakland Street, c1900s

Empire day on 24th May was established in the 1890s to celebrate the birthday of Queen Victoria and her empire and then, after her death, the day was used to promote 'good citizenship' amongst children.

Children in costume celebrating Empire Day, West Bank School, Oakland Street, c1900s

West Bank School celebrates Empire Day, 24th May, 1908

The infant school log book for that day records: *"Morning occupied with giving Empire lessons, reading St. George and the dragon, writing simple exercises and ending in a mass assembly in the playground when The Union Jack was hoisted. Photos taken."*

May Day celebrations, St. Mary's Road/White Street, c1929

"Maypoles were made and beautifully trimmed with coloured tissue paper. Often there would be a kissing bush on the top and lots of coloured ribbons hanging from it for the dancers to weave intricate patterns while they were performing around it. Money would be collected in a box."

Linda Blease, West Banker, 1930s

A West Bank celebration, Mersey Road, c1930s

The crowds are out on the streets presumably to greet the victorious Wembley Widnes Rugby League Team coming back home in 1930, given the shirt displayed on the front of the coach.

Crowds lining the street, Mersey Road, c1920s/30s

This could be the crowd waiting for the arrival of the Widnes Wembley Rugby League Team's arrival in 1930 or perhaps hoping to catch a glimpse of King George V crossing The Transporter in 1925.

Unknown West Bank Celebration, Mersey Road, c1920s/1930s

The celebrations are in full swing and people are in costume walking past The Transporter offices up Mersey Road. A band may be accompanying them since a drum can just be seen in the right hand corner.

A Street Party for V.E. Day, Oakland Street, 1945

After Winston Churchill spoke the now famous words, *"we can allow ourselves a brief period of rejoicing"*, friends, families and neighbours pooled their rationed food resources to provide a banquet for the festivities.

A Street party for V.E. Day, Oakland street, 1945

A West Bank Group on V.E Day, Oakland Street, 1945

*"West Bank streets were full of tables, chairs, music and a sense of new beginning on V.E.
Day. A lot of the streets joined together for the celebrations as the streets with aid raid
shelters were blocked off and it was difficult to have a party. I lived in Church Street and
went to the party in Cholmondeley Street."*
Ted Gleave, West Banker, 1945

Children celebrate May Day, Parsonage Road, 1953

**Tea is laid on for the children on the day that the Runcorn -Widnes
Road Bridge opened, Davies Street, 21st July1961**

**A party on the day that the Runcorn-Widnes Road Bridge opened,
James Street, 1961**

The opening of the long awaited and much needed road bridge was a cause for celebration amongst the people of West Bank.

**A street party on the day that the Runcorn-Widnes Road Bridge opened,
Davies Street, 1961**

Weddings

George and Jessie Andrews with wedding guests outside 61 and 63 Irwell Street, after their marrage at Hartland Chapel, 18th August 1915

Thomas and Constance Carolan in Church Street, after their marriage at St. Patrick's Church, 25th May 1931

Right: **John and Edith Girvin,**
 St. Mary's Church, 1931

As John Girvin was the drummer in H. Girvins celebrity dance band, it seemed fitting that the couple should walk through a guard of honour of band members and their instruments.

Left: **Herbert and Ina Cook**
 on the lawn of The
 Mersey Hotel, c1939

Joyce and Fred Hunt with wedding guest's outside St. Mary's Church, c1930s

"Father Hayes married us. We felt so privileged that he allowed us to get married at the altar. I wasn't expecting it to be so at the time. Mixed marriages took place, then, in the Vestry instead of outside in the main church."
John Garaghty, Bride Groom, 1945

Left: **The marriage of John Garaghty to Ruth Theresa Lloyd, St. Patrick's Church, 27th February 1945**

Wallace and Muriel Woods on The Prom after their marriage in St. Mary's Church, 15th June, 1948

"I remember having our wedding photographs taken in Victoria Gardens. The weather was very windy but sunny and warm. Many people arrived late to our ceremony as it was a bank holiday and it affected the buses."
Muriel Woods, Bride, 1948

Mr and Mrs Hague with wedding guests, Hartland Chapel, 23rd June 1951

Pat and Chris Turton, Best Man and Bridesmaids, St Mary's Church, 1964
Miss Pat Doyle said 'I will' to Mr Chris Turton dressed in the height of 1960s style.

**Francis Forbes marries Derek Ireland at Zion Methodist Church,
16th August 1969**

**Allison and Gordon Banner with their guests in Oakland Street,
Zion Methodist Chapel, 6th February 1977**

Chapter Five

Troubled Times

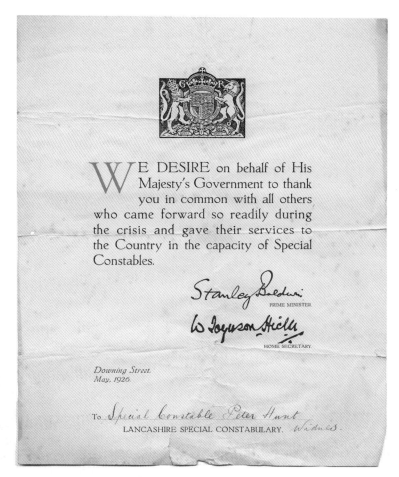

E DESIRE on behalf of His Majesty's Government to thank you in common with all others who came forward so readily during the crisis and gave their services to the Country in the capacity of Special Constables.

Stanley Baldwin
PRIME MINISTER.

W Joynson Hicks
HOME SECRETARY.

Downing Street.
May, 1926.

To *Special Constable Peter Hunt*
LANCASHIRE SPECIAL CONSTABULARY. *Widnes.*

Certificate awarded to Special Constable and West Banker Peter Hunt, 1926
The crisis referred to in this certificate is the General Strike of 1926 which was called for by the Trades Union Congress. Miners were facing a reduction in pay and support for them gathered from people in industry, railways and dockers. However, the government had made emergency measures, including the recruitment of Special Constables to deal with the situation. The General Strike ended after nine days although many miners continued striking until December when starvation forced them back to work.

ShipWrecks

A wreck of a Mersey Flat, Spike Island, c1970's

Many vessels have sunk resulting in people and animals losing their lives in the River Mersey and surrounding waterways since the area of West Bank was established. June 4th 1938 is a day etched in the minds of many West Bankers due to the tragic loss that the Horrabin family suffered at the hands of nature. A gust of wind capsized a sailing boat throwing its nineteen occupants into the water. Not all boating disasters and misadventures ended so unhappily, some of the victims were valiantly rescued by brave West Bankers. Often rescuers in the nineteenth century would be commended by organisations such as the Liverpool Shipwreck and Humane Society.

"When I was 12 just after the war it was still a time of rationing. I remember crates of corned beef being washed up on the shore alongside the promenade gardens. The corned beef had fallen off a barge which had turned over in the river just off Weston Point and the crates, which had been stored on deck, were lost overboard. When the 'alarm' was raised I joined lots of people who were wading about in the water (the tide had not gone out completely)... to my delight I stumbled across a box. I can't remember how may tins it held but it couldn't have been more than a dozen as I was able to carry it to shore myself. Many houses in Davies Street enjoyed that corned beef over the next few weeks. The police had appeared on the scene to warn people of searching for the corned beef under the penalty of fines. Too late! The 'booty' had all mysteriously disappeared!"
John Yates, West Banker, September 15th and 16th, 1947

War

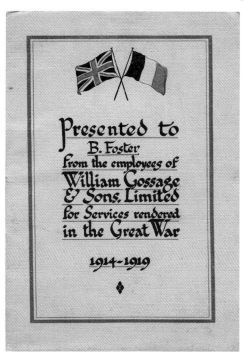

Left: **A booklet, presented to Mr Foster, listing all the men that worked for Gossgages that served in the First World War, 1919**

There was much West Bank suffering and bloodshed in both the First and Second World Wars. The Widnes Weekly News often carried reports of the tragedy that befell them. Headlines reporting the deaths of young West Bank men like Cuthbert Wilkinson (aged 21) on the 21st June 1940, *"who attended West Bank School and [was] a scholar in the Hartland Methodist Sunday School"* were all too common.

A view of the demolished British Copper Refiners Ltd. on the Dock Estate showing a Second World War Fire Watch Tower, 1960s

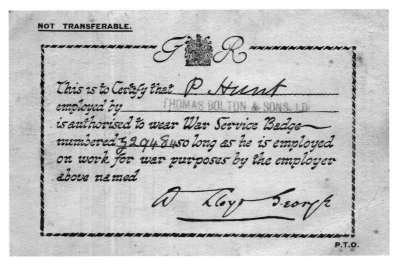

A works exemption certificate, 1916

This certificate granted an employee exclusion from being drafted into the services by stating that the holder was on necessary national work. Keeping up with the demand for munitions was crucial and many factories in Widnes were part of this effort.

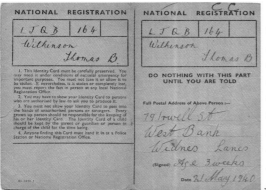

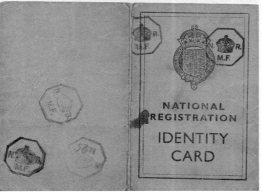

"I watched them [the German Aeroplanes] up until they got to Church Street, all lit up... there were flares and everything, it was like daylight. I watched them until they got past these, and then I said, oh, we'll have to sit and hope for the best tonight. Anyway the next thing, the bomb dropped, but where it dropped, it was a godsend. It dropped at the back of Gilmore's pub. In this side of the ICI, oh dear me, if it had gone a few yards further that way, all West Bank would have gone up."

Agnes Hunt, West Banker, 1940s

Left: **A Child's National Registration Card, 1940**

Identity cards were issued to every civilian, even if they were only three weeks old, between May 1940 and February 1952. They had to be carried at all times as proof of identity. Each card had a personal number on it.

Telegram Boys Alcuin Stephens and Dennis and Arnold Wilkinson,
Garners Garage, Mersey Road and West Bank Street c1940/1

Telegrams were delivered faster than letters during the war. However people would begin to worry at the sight of the telegram boys as they were associated with bad news.

"Telegram boys only appeared on West Bank if someone was seriously ill, was lost during the war or had died. Everyone came out from their houses if they saw a Telegram Boy to see who it was."

Leo Nolan, West Banker, 1940s

Incidents

**A Jas. Fairclough and Sons Ltd. lorry swept into housing by flooding,
St. Mary's Villas, Beamont Street, 13th August, 1956**

Faircloughs Flour Mill was hit by a thunderbolt during a storm and the downpour of rain caused the truck to be washed into the building.

Crowds gathered in the street after a water mains burst, Wright Street, c1950

Chapter Six

People

M. Lautenberg,
60. Waterloo Rd.,
Widnes.

John William Hufton, c1910's

Mr Hufton was appointed as an Assistant School Master at West Bank School from 1st September 1899 at a salary of £80 per annum. He also taught during his career at the National School in Waterloo Road.

Sarah Anne and Mary Ann Davies, Dock Street area, c1880s

Henry Hufton c1900s

Henry Hufton was the first church warden at St. Mary's Church and was also a Sunday school superintendent. He is remembered in St. Mary's church on a plaque upon one of the pillars.

Mr Thomas Herbert Nester

Mr Nestor was the first park keeper on West Bank Promenade Gardens.

"No child or anybody would dare to damage the flowers or walk on the grass, they respected him too much. It was kept and looked beautiful."

Majorie Fallon, his grandaughter, 1920s

Women and children, Beamont Street, c1908

Women and children, James Street, 1913

Girls outside 85 Mersey Road, c1900s

It is thought that these girls might be members of a sewing group, given the equipment which they are holding.

**Mary Malone,
West Bank Dock Estate, c1925**

"I used to go every week for medicine for a neighbour; Dr. Hutchinson always called me Topsey and gave me a sweet. My family had reason to be grateful to him, as all my family had the flu (epidemic during the first world war), my father died with it and Dr. Hutchinson attended us all. He didn't send my mother a bill as he knew the breadwinner had died."
Marjorie Fallon, West Banker, 1920s

Dr Hutchinson, c1920s

Jimmy Hoey, c1930s
He was one of a great many West Bank Rugby league players that brought the Chemics fame and provided a great deal of pleasure to those who followed the game

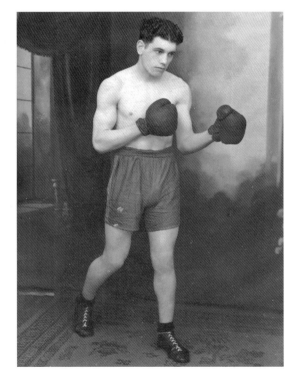

Pat Ryan, Boxer, 1940s
Pat lived and trained on West Bank.

Left: Frank Cox, 1940's

Frank was a teacher then deputy head at St. Patrick's School (1936-46) as well as a Scout Master and a talented organist at St. Patrick's Church. Both Frank and his wife, Doris, served the community throughout their lives becoming highly regarded amongst West Bankers.

A group including, Frank and Doris Cox and Frank Moran, St. Patrick's School, Dock Street, 1930s

Annie Thomas, Mrs Joyson, Joyce Youd and Nellie Youd, White Street, c1935

Tommy, David and Laura Ellis and a friend, 12 Irwell Street, c1940s

Janet and Margaret Wilkinson,
Viaduct Street, late 1940s early 1950s

Mrs Dolan and Mrs Heneghan,
St. Mary's Road, c1950s

Emma McMullen, a teacher at West Bank School, Oakland Street, c1940s

West Bankers, Pitt Street field, c1952

**Thelma Wareing, her mother Margaret Wareing and her grandmother
Margaret Wareing, The Bridge Hotel, corner of Viaduct and Church Street, c1950**

A lady with two small girls, Hurst Street, 1950s

Arthur Atherton, Bridge Street looking eastwards, c1960

Chapter Seven

Childhood

**Linda Kilshaw, Edward Lamb,Vera Kilshaw holding Teddy
the dog and Eunice Kilshaw, 1 West Street, c1929**

West Bank School

A boys' woodwork class, West Bank School, c1900s

Boys of Standard 3, West Bank School, c1910s

Lessons were not always taken in the classroom. On 23 March 1906 a West Bank School log book records that *"Class 1 were taken by class teacher to promenade gardens for observation lesson on the sun and its effects."*

The girls of Standard 5, West Bank School, 1915

An entry in The West Bank School Log Book, written by the Head Teacher in 1915 reads *"The teachers have not insisted upon the use of thimbles during the needlework lessons - have therefore replenished the classes with same throughout the school and given orders for their regular use."*

School Girls, West Bank School, c1920

"I was known by the teachers as 'The Pied Piper' of West Bank School. I'd get fed up with lessons and sneak out of school through a gap in the gate little people could get through. By the time I got down to The Prom there were a dozen children behind me!" Bessy O'Brien, West Bank School Pupil, 1920s

Girls from West Bank School, Oakland Street, c1927

Children having a celebration at West Bank School, c1930s

Class 3 with Mr Stirrup and Miss Townsend, West Bank School, c1947/48

**Standard 2 with Mr Johnson, Mr Stirrup and Mrs Carter,
West Bank School, c1948/49**

Standard 1A with Mr Stirrup and Miss Peddar, West Bank School, c1947

Standard 4A with Mr Stirrup and Mr Humpreys, c1949

**Standard 4B with Mr Stirrup and Miss Townsend,
West Bank School, c1951/2**

**West Bank girls who had passed the
eleven plus to attend Wade Deacon,
West Bank School yard, June 1952**
Back row from left to right: Alison Gerrard,
Barbara Beswick, Madge Smitham, Front
row Maureen Brooks and Gwen Hackney.

**A school report from West Bank School,
1957**

West Bank School girls' athletics team with a trophy, West Bank School, 1960

Girls with scales, West Bank School, c1960s

St. Patrick's School

School girls in a classroom at St. Patrick's School, 1910s

"Each child would be given a sewing needle to last the whole year. The teacher had to supply replacement needles for those lost down the dusty worn floorboards. Each piece of tacking thread had to be carefully removed and placed over pegs that held the slate board. These pieces of thread were used over and over again."
Kathleen Graham, Teacher at St. Patrick's School, 1922

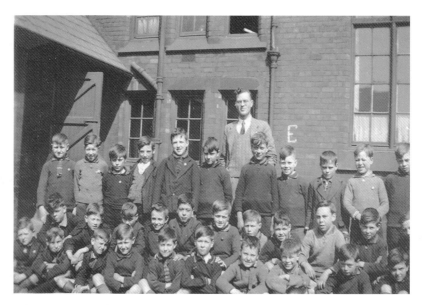

School boys in the yard of St. Patrick's School with their teacher, Frank Cox, 1940s

Teachers from St. Patrick's School, 1941

On the back row are Miss Mulroy and Miss Rimmer, whilst at the front are headmaster Mr Hunt and Mr Cox. These teachers would have taught St. Patrick's pupils mathematics, reading, english (literature, recitation and grammar), writing and composition, history and geography, science, music, drawing and needlework. They also taught P.T. and 'hand and eye training'.

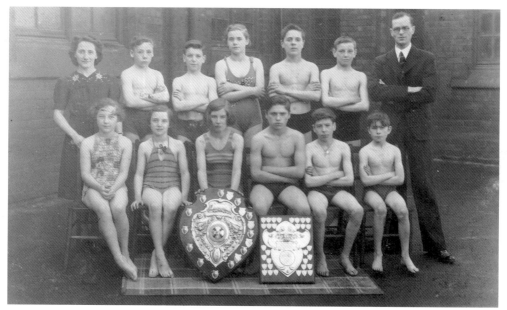

The swimming team, St. Patrick's School, 1942

The swimming team, St. Patrick's School, 1944

The swimming team, St. Patrick's School, 1946

Children dancing around a maypole at St. Patrick's School, 1970s

A school reunion for pupils of St. Patrick's School, 1970s

School Days, Friends and Trips

The National School, Waterloo Road, c1914

Children, teachers and Reverend Albert Swain at the National School, Waterloo Road, c1950

Children in the school yard in what is thought to be The National School, 1910s

Nursery School Children, West Bank Nursery, West Bank School c1944

School friends from West Bank School on a day out, 1920s

St. Mary's Sunday School anniversary trip, West Bank, c1957
"The Sunday School anniversary was very special and everyone seemed to have a 'Sunday best' outfit for the occasion... We were taken on an annual treat either to Frodsham Hill or out on a farm in Halebank. We had a small sports session and a picnic tea sitting on the grass."
Linda Kilshaw, West Banker, 1930s

Children from Hartland Sunday School Youth Club, 1950s
In 1926 and 1927 the Hartland Sunday School log book records that they had their annual treat to Runcorn Pleasure Grounds. The following year in July they went to Halebank.

A school trip, West Bank School, Southport, 1940s

At Play

From left to right: Charlie, Lucy, Mary and Tom McGloin, 33 Pitt Street, c1914

From left to right: Kate, Margaret and Jane Malone, 66a Oakland Street, 1915

Childhood friends from Davies Street, 1920s

**Ina Booth playing on railings on
The Promenade, c1930s**

Girls also played sovereigns or sovs.
*"We depended on finding pieces of pottery
or china with gold edging or gold lines on
it and we would shop to barter for better
pieces with 'the goods' laid out on an
upturned wooden orange box."*
Linda Kilshaw, West Banker 1930s

Ina Booth, West Bank, c1930

Children, Oakland Street, c1940s

Left: **Joyce and Ken Rowlinson,
34 White Street, 1948**
Bicycles and tricycles were very precious possessions on West Bank as not every child had one.
"At every opportunity we would borrow an unattended bike, thereby we could learn to ride, it was easy downwards but an effort to ride up the slope of James Street."
Bill Foster, West Banker, 1930s

**Maureen and Wendy Garner,
West Street, c1946/47**

**Peter, John, Barbara and Brian Kelly
outside 23 St. Mary's Road, 1940's**
"With little transport there was very little to stop us playing in the streets. Everyone had a skipping rope, lads and girls all joining in a line with french skipping."
Bill Foster, West Banker, 1930s.

Friends outside the Bridge Hotel, junction of Viaduct and Church Street, 1949/50
From left to right back row: Ronnie Jones, Graham Baxter and George Wareing. Front row: AlanWoods, David Baxter and Jack Ellis.

Young people, West Bank Street, c1945

Pauline Cox, 67 Irwell Street, c1950

**Wendy Garner on the forecourt of
Garner's Garage, Mersey Road, c1947**

Peter Cox, Victoria Gardens, c1950

Peter Canning and Doris Grundy, Parsonage Road, c1950/1951

**Left: Elsie and Eddie Jones,
The Marshes, 1950's**

Children also played on the marshes, 'the cut' and the docks despite being forbidden by their parents to do so. These areas were fraught with the dangers of open water and the hustle and bustle of industry.
"I used to spend a lot of my time with the engines riding up and down West Bank Dock."
Jack Wickham, West Banker, 1920s

**Ivy Tomlinson,
Back yard of 79 Irwell Street, c1952**
Many West Bankers can remember going home for lunch from school.
"Each dinner time I would rush home from School, collect my father's wicker lunch box and run to the gate of the works, standing with others I knew on the same mission."
Bill Foster, West Banker, 1930s.

**Pauline Cox on a climbing frame,
Victoria Park, c1950s**
Children often got together and organised their own games of cricket and rounders.
" You had only to hit the ball up towards Irwell Street. The boundaries would be four window sills, two on each side of the road, four or five houses apart."
Bill Foster, West Banker, 1930s

**John and Tommy Wilkinson on board 'The Mary Ellen',
lock gates, Spike Island, 1950s**

Boys playing football in the street, photographed by Gordon Gilray, Terrace Road, c1970s

Children collecting for a bonfire photographed by Gordon Gilray, Terrace Road, October 1975

"At bonfire time we used to collect all the old timber... The shops backyards were a big help in storing the makings for our fire. All the shops had sheds and stored boxes within... The owners enjoyed November 5th as much as we did."
Bill Foster, West Banker, 1930s

The Boys Brigade

**Boys from the 1st Widnes Boys Brigade Company founded in 1884,
pictured on camp at the Isle of Man, 1897**

The 2nd Widnes Boys Brigade Company, The National School Yard, 1927
After the 1st World War the company reformed as the 2nd Widnes Boys Brigade.

**The 2nd Widnes Company Boys Brigade Band,
The National School Yard, c1925**

**The 2nd Widnes Boys Brigade Company Band marching to celebrate the
arrival of St. Mary's Church Rose Queen, Irwell Street, 1950**

Tommy Davies, pictured with the other members of the band, tightens up the big drum back stage in the Tin Mission, Davies Street, 1952

The 2nd Widnes Boys Brigade Company Band on parade, Bank Street, c1950s

An annual photograph of the 2nd Widnes Boys Brigade Company at the end of the winter session, St. Mary's Parochial Hall, 1960-1

Raymond Crew and Eric Wilson together with Lieutenant John Yates demonstrate canoe making at a recuitment exhibition in the grounds of the old St. Mary's Church known as 'The Black', 1963

The 2nd Widnes Company receive news of the Boys Brigade camp, 1955

**An advance party of 2nd Widnes Boys Brigade depart for camp,
Davies Street, 1961**

The 2nd Widnes Boys Brigade Company win the five-a-side championships, 1972

**The 2nd Widnes Boys Brigade Company annual photograph,
St. Mary's Parochial Hall, 1973**

Bownies, Guides and Scouts

**The 7th Widnes (St. Mary's Scouts) on the lawn of the Vicarage,
Parsonage Road, 1919**

This scout troop replaced the Boys Brigade on West Bank for a number of years between 1914 and 1925.

**The 2nd Widnes (St. Mary's) Guides about to set off on a
trip outside St. Mary's Church, Beamont Street, c1950s**

The 2nd Widnes (St. Mary's) Guides, from left to right: Valerie Burgess, Jean Combes, Kathleen McCormack, Gwyneth Fisher and Coleen Davies, 74 Davies Street, c1963/4

The 2nd Widnes (St. Mary's) Brownies, The Parochial Hall, Davies Street, 1970s

The 2nd Widnes (St. Mary's) Brownies, Beamont Street, 1970s

"When I was in the Brownies, we met in the Tin Mission and then later the Brownies met in the Parochial Hall when that was built. Mrs Cheshire [Brown Owl] believed in children enjoying themselves so we would play lots of games as well as work for badges."
Eunice Stobbie, 2nd Widnes (St. Mary's Brownies), 1930's

Boys from the 17th Widnes (St. Patrick's) Scout Group with their Scout leader, Frank Cox, location unknown, 1938

These boys were chosen as a guard of honour for the visit of King George VI and Queen Elizabeth on May 9th 1938.

Left: Boys from the 17th Widnes (St. Patrick's) Scout Group travelling to or from camp, location unknown, 1940s

Like the Boys Brigade company on West Bank the highlight of the year was participating in the annual camp which was often held in Wales or the Lake District.

Girls from the 13th Widnes (St.Patrick's) Girl Guides, Church Street, 1940s

This Guide Troop from St. Patrick's Church are participating in a St. Georges Day parade. St Patrick's Presbytery, St. Patrick's School and the railway viaduct are behind them.

Chapter Eight

Trade

Joseph Penketh outside his shop, Penketh's Grocers, Church Street, 1940
"Mrs Ashton ran a drapers shop and she used to sell penny balls of wool in every colour under the sun. There were so many shops in West Bank."
Mrs M. Gilhooley, West Banker, 1920s

Mersey Road Shops

Above: **The Maypole Dairy Company, Mersey Road, c1927**

Left: **The Maypole Dairy Company and staff, Mersey Road, 1950s**

"As I was the 'last in' it was my job to scrub the floor at the end of each day. It was a beautiful floor of green and brown tiles, with the maypole pattern in the middle."
Maureen Taylor, Shop Assistant, The Maypole, 1950s

A.C. Wright, butchers, 22 Mersey Road, c1920's
"My brother Dennis and I used to have an after-school job at this shop putting the links into sausages."
Maureen Taylor, West Banker, 1940s

Staff outside the Co-op, Mersey Road, 1950s
The Co-op was the fourth branch in Widnes and next door to it was Mrs McCloud's hat shop.

George Parnell, Mersey Road, 1950s

This was the first 'self service' shop in Widnes.

"As a child I used to take a dish on a Tuesday to Parnell's and collect 'savoury ducks'.
People would queue up from 4pm."
John Moss, West Banker, 1940s

The meat counter, George Parnell, Mersey Road,1950s

W.H. Garner, wine shop, Mersey Road, c1950s

"This shop not only sold wine but tabacco and cigarettes. There was a white form for people to sit on, I don't know why as I never saw anyone sitting on it! Behind the Counter were the wines and tobacco."

Maureen Taylor, West Banker, 1950s

Fanny Garner, proprietor, W.H. Garner, wine shop, Mersey Road, c1960

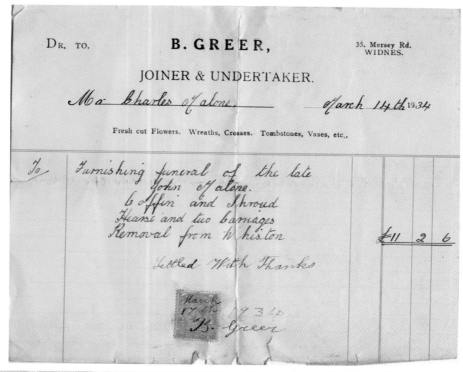

Dr. to. B. GREER,
35, Mersey Rd.
WIDNES.

JOINER & UNDERTAKER.

Mr Charles Malone, March 14th 1934

Fresh cut Flowers. Wreaths, Crosses. Tombstones, Vases, etc.,

To Furnishing funeral of the late
John Malone.
Coffin and Shroud
Hearse and two Carriages
Removal from Whiston £11 2 6

Settled With Thanks

March 17th 1934
B. Greer

Above: **A receipt from Greer, Joiners and Undertakers, Mersey Road, 1934**

"Children used to shout "any empty boxes?" as they passed Greer's."
Bessy O'Brien, West Banker, 1920s

Left: **Reginald Sherratt Haircutting and Shaving Saloon, 49 Mersey Road, c1920s**
Mr Sherratt also repaired umbrellas.

Left: **Stuart Haughton's Newsagents,
next to the Mersey Hotel, 1940s**
*"Being the nearest newsagent to The Trans-
porter Bridge much of Mr Haughton's trade
resulted from those that used it"*
John Harper, West Banker, 1950s

Below: **The Newsagents run by Jean
Mottram, junction of Mersey
Road and Bank Street, 1976**

Waterloo Road and Dock Street Shops

An envelope for newly developed photographs,
Mark Lautenburg, Photographers, 60, Waterloo Road, c1940s

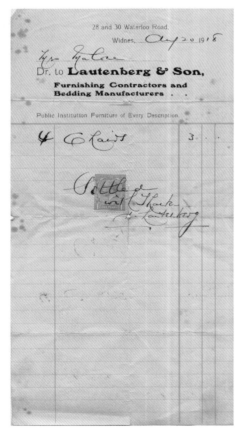

A reciept from Lautenburg and Son,
41 Waterloo Road, 1918

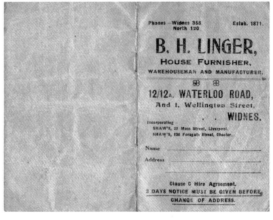

A payment book from B. H Linger,
12/12a Waterloo Road, c1930s

J. Gaddick's shop, Waterloo Road c1930

This shop sold sweets and tobacco.

People outside what is presumed to be the grocer's shop run by Mrs Hoey, Dock Street, c1920s

Briget and JimmyWeir are pictured with their son Georgie and another lady.

Shops in other West Bank streets

Mrs Julia O'Brien and baby outside Roberts, Church Street, 1950s
Roberts sold ladies' clothes and Robinsons, a general shop, was next door to it.

Nucky Wood's Shop, corner of West Street and Church Street, c1950s
This shop sold sweets, cigarettes, pop and was a general grocery shop.

154

Robinson's shop doorway, junction of Church Street and Wright Street, 1920s

Frederick Bishop Decorators, 5 Oakland Street, c1900s

A card for Turtons Artistic Photography, West Bank, early 20th Century

Chapter Nine

Industry

Certificate for 40 years service from Thomas Bolton and Sons Ltd.
West Banker Peter Hunt joined Boltons in 1909 and began work as a general labourer, in the 'Dolfin' Building and eventually became a plumber's mate.

William Gossage and Sons Ltd.

Women Workers at William Gossage and Sons Ltd., Mersey Road, 1900s
These Workers at Gossages in clogs and work attire are, from left, Mrs A. Clarke, Mrs
Furber, Mrs Spruce, Mrs Pennington and Mrs Combes. Women were employed at Gos-
sages mainly as soap packers.

**Two firemen outside the Fire Station of William Gossage and Sons Ltd.,
Mersey Road, c1920s**
William Wimpenny, right, and colleague pose for a photograph.

**Ellen Emma Stokes, worker at William Gossage and Sons Ltd., Mersey Road,
photograph taken at M. Lautenburg's Studio, Waterloo Road, c1909**
*"The women had to wash their own overalls at home and so often let a few
shavings [of soap] fall into their pockets to help with the weekly wash."*
Bessie O' Brien, West Banker, 1920s

Workers at Jas. Fairclough and Sons, St. Mary's Road, c1900

TELEPHONE : 385 WIDNES. TELEGRAMS : "FAIRCLOUGHS"

Jas. Fairclough & Sons Ld.
West Bank Corn Mills,
Widnes.

REGISTERED OFFICE & FLOUR MILLS AT WARRINGTON.

Presented by W. H. Wilcock.

A business card for Jas. Fairclough and Sons, St Mary's Road, early 20th Century

.... *19*

FLOUR

Dreadnought	...	...	...	280 lbs.
Sanitas	...	...	...	"
D. Super	...	...	...	"
Super	...	...	...	"
Best Seconds	...	...	...	"
F. B. Meal (Brown Flour)	...			"
Self-Raising	...	...	...	doz. lbs.

MILL OFFALS

Thirds	...	...	...	112 lbs.
Bran	...	...	...	"
B. Y. Bran	...	...	...	"

"At certain times of the day, they used to let the gas out [of the factories] and it did smell. It was mostly in a morning and it used to be like a fog, and everywhere was so dirty after it had diminished. It used to get into our throats and make us cough... but we lived through it, well we had to, or else have no money."
Marjorie Fallon, West Banker, 1920s

Max Bernstein's

**Workers from Max Bernstein's at a presentation ceremony,
Hutchinson Street, 1950s**

'The Shirt Factory' as it was commonly known made not only shirts but also pyjamas and blouses for companies such as Marks and Spencer.

Workers from Max Bernstein's, Hutchinson Street, 1950s

There was also a 'bag factory' in West Bank and J. Hurst and Sons was known as the 'Slipper Factory'. Hurst made uppers for shoes from the old Trinity Church building in Waterloo Road.

"Machinists were paid per piece produced and therefore we learnt how to fix our own machines quickly."

Megan Jones, Worker at J. Hurst and Sons, Waterloo Road, 1958 -1961

Cooper's Mineral Works

**Alf Burgess (left) and Stuart Berry at Cooper's Mineral Works,
St. Mary's Road, c1940**

Alf joined the company, established in 1905, straight from school at 14 and stayed until
Mr Arthur Cooper sold it in the 1940s.

*"At the factory the number of workers employed was twelve; six of them working with
the lorries and one with the horse and cart. The two men who bottled the drinks and
filled the siphons of soda were grand chaps and taught me a lot of things regarding the
job."*

Alf Burgess, Worker at Cooper's Mineral Works, 1937-44

West Bank Power Station and ICI

A retirement presentation for Jack Birch at West Bank Power Station, 1949
The power station was built in 1929 and closed in the early 1960s.

**Cecilia Carolan, Mary Marr and Theresa Carolan outside the Central Laboratory
Research and Development Offices of ICI, off Waterloo Road, c1955**
Theresa was a secretary to a senior manager at this part of ICI, for around 15 years from
1952 when she started at the age of 14.

William Cooper and Sons Ltd. and The Birmingham Metal Company

Workers from William Cooper and Sons Ltd., St. Mary's Road, c1900's
Fred Roscaleer is pictured on the back row fourth from the right.

Workers at William Cooper and Sons Ltd., St. Mary's Road, 1950s
These men were employed as riggers and general labourers, apprentice fitters, ship wrights, marine fitters or turners at Coopers. There were also blacksmiths, office staff, store keepers, and marine engineers employed at the shipyard.

Workers at William Cooper and Sons Ltd., St Mary's Road, 1950

From right to left: Frank Atkin, Jim Keogh, Ken Barlow and Wallace Woods outside the Engine Shed Workshop at William Coopers.

" In the fitting room there were workman's benches that ran the length of the shop with numerous vices, under which were drawers for tools to carry out work with and so forth. There were also two grinding machines used for sharpening up drill bits and lathe tools for metal."

Wallace Woods, Marine Engineer, 1950s

Workers, The Birmingham Metal Company, West Bank Dock Estate c1938

Gaskell–Marsh

Above: **A Presention at Gaskell-Marsh, West Bank Dock Estate, 1951**

Left: **Workers outside the Fire Station at Gaskell-Marsh, c1950s**

Thomas Bolton and Sons Ltd

Workers at Thomas Bolton and Sons Ltd., Hutchinson Street, 1940s
Laurence Greenwood, pictured on the front row first left, was a furnace man at the Mersey Copper Works from 1947-53 shovelling coal into the furnace. The works were set up to roll and smelt copper in 1880 in Widnes.

Work on the roof, Thomas Bolton and Son's, Hutchinson Street, c1958
Eric Smith carries out repair work on the roof at the 'Dolfin' building of the works. Each of the buildings had a colloquial name and the others were called 'The Blue' and 'The Green after the colours of the chemicals used in them.

Eric Smith sat on one of the storage tanks inside the 'Dofin' Building whilst completing a maintenance task, Thomas Bolton and Sons Ltd., c1958

Many people got jobs or apprenticeships through family and friends so it often meant that two or more generations of the same family could be employed at the same place of work. Eric Smith's grandfather, who worked at Boltons from the age of eighteen in 1900 until 1950, got him his job with the firm.

"When you started a job after school you got an indenture. You promised to stay with that company through your apprenticeship until you were 21 and they promised to give you work."
Eric Smith, Joiner, Thomas Bolton and Sons, 1949-62

Left: **Eric Smith outside the canteen, Thomas Bolton and Son's Ltd., Hutchinson Street, 1950s**

Eric Hunt, Hughy Nocton and Mr Proctor,
Thomas Boltons and Sons Ltd., Hutchinson Street, 1940s

The chimneys of the boiler house on the site and the railway viaduct can be seen behind them.

Copper ingots weighing aprroximately 28lb each,
Thomas Bolton and Sons, Hutchinson Street, 1950s

A view of Thomas Bolton and Sons Ltd., Hutchinson Street, 1960s

British Copper Refiners Limited, Hutchinson Street, October 1965
This building was orginally part of Thomas Bolton and Sons before it was taken over by BCR Ltd. in 1962.

Chapter Ten

The Docks

George Andrews, West Bank Dock, c1910s

George worked at William Gossage and Sons Ltd. but is photographed on the docks dressed in his bowler hat and suit. West Bank Dock was constructed by John Hutchinson in 1864 and remained in use until the late 1950s.

Widnes Dock labourers, Widnes Dock, c1900s
Widnes Docks opened in 1862 and these men worked hard loading and unloading cargoes
and carrying out general labouring work.

St. Helen's Canal and lock keepers cottages, Widnes Dock, c1900s
Mr Axford the lock keeper is photographed next to the cottage he lived in and worked
alongside. It was owned by the railway company. In the 1940's Mr Billy Riley was the
lock keeper and lived with his two sons in the house.

The lock gates to St. Helens Canal, Widnes Dock, c1900s

Now located on the tranquil Spike Island these lock gates were in constant use before the 1950's to transport goods to and from Manchester.

The house belonging to the Dock Warden, Widnes Dock, c1900s

In the early days of the chemical industry most of the housing development was centred on Spike Island, rather than 'true' West Bank as that was where all the work was. One of the theories of how Spike Island got it's name relates to the fact that a 'spike' was a cheap boarding house of the kind that would have been plentiful around the factories.

The railway crossing over St. Helens Canal, Widnes Dock, 1950s
The railways ran next to the wharves and the extensive network meant that goods could be moved to any of the works that ran alongside the St. Helens canal without more unloading than was necessary.

**The locomotive 'Reliance' operated by ICI West Bank Power Station,
West Bank Dock Estate, c1950s**

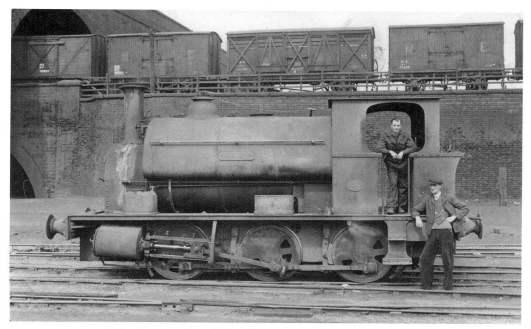

The locomotive 'Mary', West Bank Dock, c1940s

Of the locomotives that ran on West Bank Dock four of them were named after estate owner Mr Hutchinson's daughters. Mary is pictured above and the others were Gertrude, Lucy and Margaret. Gossage's had 'fireless' locomotives which were powered by high pressure steam

The locomotive 'Sir Holbrook', ICI Gaskell-Marsh Works, West Bank Dock Estate, c1950s

**The locomotive 'The Magadi', ICI West Bank Power Station,
West Bank Dock, c1950s**

*"We would go onto the Huchinson Docks
[as children] with sacks and pick up
lumps of coal, which had spilled onto the
railway lines, sometimes from the wagons
as well. We had to be smartish to dodge
the railway police."*
Bill Foster, West Banker, 1930s

Left: **View of West Bank Dock from
the Runcorn-Widnes Road
Bridge as it was nearing
completion, 1961**

'The Pilot', West Bank Dock, c1900s

Moored off West Bank Dock, The Pilot was a working boat used to safely guide others laden with goods into the dock, by navigating them through the shallow waters.

Jack Fallows and a colleague on what is thought to be a boat belonging to William Cooper and Sons Ltd., Widnes Dock, c1960

Chapter Eleven

The Mersey

Boats anchored on the shore, The River Mersey, c1940s

A boat on the River Mersey, c1960

**Kenny Jackson and Jo Sorville on board the shrimping boat
'The Gentle Annie', the River Mersey, c1950s**

The barrel for boiling the shrimps can be seen in the foreground. The amount of boiling time and the quantity of salt added to the water could effect the taste of the shrimps and people strove to perfect their recipes.

"The river was a very busy river with all the yachts and shrimp boats, as West Bank was known for its shrimps. As the shrimp boats came in people were queuing to take them all over the town and outside it. After that the village would go quiet as everybody was schulling shrimps to pot and sell and go out with their wares."
Marjorie Fallon, West Banker, 1930s

Chapter Twelve

The Bridges

**Doris Cox, right, and friends using the footpath on the
Ethelfleda Railway Bridge, 1937**

The Railway Bridge

The Ethelfleda Railway Bridge, before 1905

Prior to any bridge a ferry enabled people to cross The Mersey. It had been in existence since medieval times but the crossing could be extremely hazardous. The first permanent structure was the railway bridge which opened in May 1868.

"I often used the footbridge to go to dances in Runcorn in the early 1930s. When a train went over the whole bridge shook. In the war there were sentries stationed at each end of the bridge to find out whether the person crossing was a friend or foe."
Marjorie Fallon, West Banker, 1930s

**An aeriel view of The Ethelfleda Railway Bridge with the
ICI Power Station in the background c.1930s/40s**

Ann Sumner, crossing by foot on The Ethelfleda Railway Bridge, c1960

The Transporter Bridge

A steam traction engine moving parts of the Transporter Bridge, which were used to fasten the structure onto the bed rock, c1904

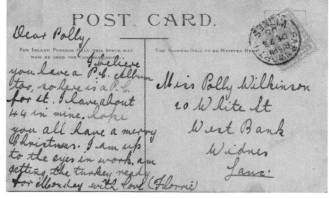

A postcard sent to Polly Wilkinson living at 20 White Street, celebrating Christmas 1905.
The Transporter Bridge opened on May 29th 1905. The imposing structure became a national landmark and was a frequently used image on postcards

Left: **A close up view of the Transporter Bridge from the Promenade, 1950s**

The Engineers' Workshop together with the Suspended Carriage, often called the Transporter Car, can be seen clearly in this magnificient piece of Edwardian engineering.

"There used to be gangs of lads shouting for people to throw a halfpenny down usually on a Thursday and Friday when people got paid. They would all then challenge each other to retrieve the money from the bottom of the Mersey"
Jimmy Lee, West Banker, 1940s

The approach to The Transporter, Mersey Road, 1950s
Buses would pull up around the building on the left and reverse backwards towards The Transporter.
"The drivers often used The Transporter Offices on the corner of Mersey Road and St. Mary's Road for their breaks."
Jimmy Lee, West Banker, 1928-65

The Transporter Car in motion, 1959
The journey over the Mersey only took a matter of minutes but throughout its 58 year life span it was often unreliable and could be shut down especially if the winds were high.

The Transporter toll booth photographed on the last day the Transporter was in operation, 22nd July 1961

Crowds gather to see the final journey of The Transporter car, Mersey Road, 1961

Souvenir Ticket for the last trip on the Transporter Bridge

The very last trip that the Transporter made was for invited guests and commemorative tickets were issued

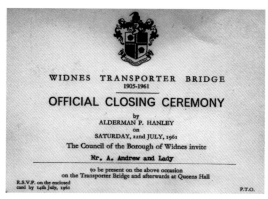

The Transporter Bridge Closing Ceremony Invitation

The Transporter closed the day after the Runcorn-Widnes Road Bridge opened.

The Transporter Car docked at West Bank, 22nd July 1961

George Done, who had been employed in the operation of the Transporter Bridge, witnesses the last trip, 1961

The Road Bridge

**The supports for the Runcorn-Widnes Road Bridge
which replaced housing in Viaduct Street, c1960**

**The construction of the approach road as seen from
the Ethelfleda Railway Bridge footpath, c1960**

Construction of the Runcorn-Widnes Road Bridge between the existing Railway and Transporter Bridges c.1960

The Runcorn-Widnes Road Bridge begins to take shape as viewed from the jetty alongside the Mersey Hotel, c1960

**The main span of the bridge nearing completion
as viewed from The Promenade, c1960**

**The bird's eye view that the construction workers
had working on The Runcorn -Widnes Road Bridge, c1960**

21st July 1961- Opening Day

**The Runcorn-Widnes Road Bridge
in use, 21st July 1961**

There was orginally a footpath on both sides
of the road and there were no safety barriers
for protection.

**The Road Bridge approach road on
the day that the bridge opened, 1961**

WIDNES

Collette Cox, standing on The Runcorn-Widnes Road Bridge, July 1961

Above: **A lorry preparing to unload timber
baulks during the widening of
the road bridge, February 1975**
Right: **The road bridge before it was
widened, February 1975**

The approach road to the bridge prior to work to widen it, February, 1975
The works on the bridge finished in August 1977 and to commemorate 25 years of Queen
Elizabeth II's reign it was renamed The Silver Jubilee Bridge.

Chapter Thirteen

Transport

Janet Wilkinson on a paratrooper's motorcycle, Irwell Street, c1948/9

A Widnes Commer Bus, junction of Church Street and Viaduct Street, c1911

Left: **A Widnes Commer Bus, Viaduct Street, c1910**

In 1909 Widnes boasted four Commer Buses, the first covered top buses in Engand, and the bus timetable included transporting people to and from West Bank.

"Every Saturday night there used to be a wagonette which would go from The Angel Hotel, it was Suttons Pub then... you could go to the market then and pick up all the bargains after nine o'clock... There was a coach which used to run on a night-time which went to Hale Shore."

Lucy Jones and Jack Wickham, West Bankers, 1920s

Left: **A delivery to
The Swan Public
House,
Waterloo Road,
late 1950s**

Ina Booth on a motorbike, Mersey Road, c1930s

There was a Widnes Motorcycle Club and West Bankers like Mr. T. Lewis, pictured on page 40, were certainly members. In the 1920s and 1930s motorcycling became a fashionable pastime throughout the country.

David Mercer riding a bicycle down James Street, 1940s

A bus waiting for the Transporter Car to dock, Mersey Road c1950s

Chapter Fourteen

Places

**The house occupied by the dock warden decorated for the Coronation
of Edward VII, St Helens Canal, Spike Island, 1901**

On the Mersey Shore

The bandstand, Victoria Gardens, c1900s

The orginal promenade was extended and the bandstand built in commemoration of Queen Victoria and it was opened on 21st May 1903.

"There used to be bands that played in The Promenade, Sunday nights after church in particular."
Bessy O'Brien, West Banker, 1920s

A view of West Bank before the current St. Mary's Church was built, St Mary's Road c1900s

Houses in Beamont Street and St. Mary's Road were demolished to build the new church.

A view of the Promenade after the construction of St. Mary's Church, c1910s

Victoria Gardens, c1900s

In the foreground of this photograph is the Park Keeper's Hut where the groundsmen, such as Mr Stocker in the 1920s and 30s, used to keep their tools

St. Mary's Parsonage, Parsonage Road, c1900s

The first St. Mary's Parsonage was buried in the embankment for the Railway Bridge in the 19th Century and the replacement vicarage, photographed above, was constructed facing the river.

The Accident Hospital entrance way, St Mary's Road, 1970s

The Hospital opened in 1878 to serve the emerging community.

"Well, we used to go and visit [my brother] and when you went in the waiting room you had to change your shoes, put slippers on to go into the wards."

Jack Wickham, West Banker 1920s

West Bank Buildings

West Bank School, Cholmondeley Street, c1920s
The school opened in July 1877.

The West Bank Power Station, West Bank Dock, 1970s
The Power station was built c1929 and closed in the mid 1960s

The Mersey Hotel, Mersey Road, c1900s

Also known as 'The Snig Pie House', The Mersey Hotel was famous for eel pies which were caught in the Mersey. In the foreground can be seen the bowling green with a game being watched by the crowds.

A public house run by John Campbell (pictured),
Church Street, c1900s

The Arch Hotel, corner of Lower Church Street and Dock Street, c1900s

"I used to go for my Sunday dinner there sometimes and I would be walking through sawdust and spittoons."

Jack Wickham, West Banker, 1930's

The Bridge Hotel, corner of Viaduct Street and Church Street, 1955

The Bridge Hotel was also known as 'The Round House'. The pub was a very prominent building on West Bank not least because of its curved frontage.

The White Star Hotel, corner of Pear Street and West Bank Street, c1960s
Popular Lollipop Lady Mrs Reardon and her dog can be seen assisting the children to cross the road safely.
"As kids we would often stand on the pub window sills to see if our fathers were inside!"
Ste Lee, West Banker, 1960's

Irwell Street c1955
The folk of West Bank have come out to watch the mayor, in his car, leaving the Hartland Chapel.

The construction of St. Patrick's Club, Dock Street, 1930s

Left: **St. Patrick's Church, Dock Street, c1950s**
This view is taken from St. Mary's Cemetery, after the headstones were removed and the graves grassed over, some time before the 1960s.

"St. Patrick's Church was an institution dear to the heart of many West Bankers. It had fine sandstone pillars, statues and lots of marble. At the entrance and altar were beautiful stained glass windows of St. Patrick with the snakes at his feet. When the last mass was held in the church many people were very tearful."
Eric Hunt, West Banker, 1990s

The 'Big House', junction of Beamont Street and Irwell Street c1975

Davies Street, c1970s

Chapter Fifteen

Redevelopment

James Street, c1970s

This photograph was taken from the roof of 106 Hurst Street. Today James Street, like Davies Street and Hurst Street and many others, are no longer in existence as the 19th century terraces were swept away in the process of the redevelopment of West Bank in the mid 1970s.

"Photographing the demolition of the old Century cinema brought back wartime memo-
ries for me of the air raid shelter that was just to the left of it. I took my daughter to see the
house where I had grown up in, which was in Oakland Street. I felt like another part of my
life had gone. West Bank just wasn't the same as when I was a lad."
Ron Cank, West Banker, 1970's

**Demolition in Viaduct Street making way for
The Runcorn-Widnes Road Bridge, 1959**

**A crowd watches as the foundation stone for the new vicarage is laid,
St. Mary's Road, 5th July 1958**

St. Mary's Vicarage located in Parsonage Road was one of the first buildings to be domolished to make way for the road bridge.

Laying the foundation stone for the new vicarage, 5th July 1958

The new vicarage takes shape, 1958

Street clearance, Bank Street and Davies Street area in foreground, 1970s
The once familiar James and Irwell Streets have gone from behind Gladys, Tracey and
Tom Mottram who are walking along Bank Street. The Britannia or 'Blood Tub' can be
seen in the background.

**A JCB moving earth in the Davies Street, Beamont and
Irwell Street area as viewed from Bank Street, 1970s**

**The intial stages of constructing the new houses
as viewed from Bank Street, 1970s**

Construction of new houses, taken from Bank Street, 1970s

Land clearance for new houses in Terrace Road, 1970s

**The day that the new road was officially opened,
Terrace Road, 24th September 1975**

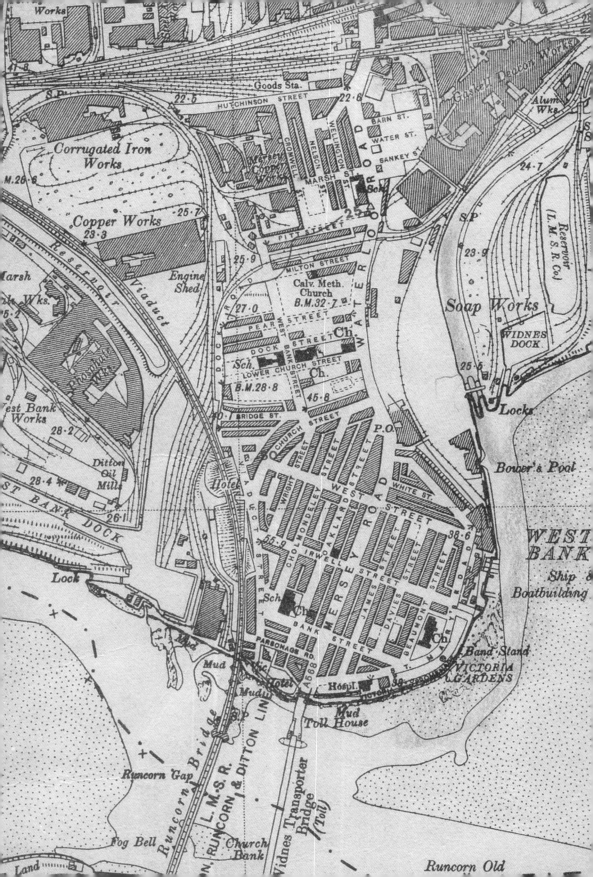